Good Sense & the Faithless

GOOD
&SENSE
the Faithless

poems by Michélle T. Clinton

West End Press

Grateful acknowledgment is made to the following publications in which some of these poems originally appeared:

Ache; Amnesia; Caffeine; Cups; Enclitic; Fast Talk, Full Volume; Gargoyle; Harbinger; Helter Skelter, L.A. Art in the '90s; High Performance Magazine; Invocation L.A.; Kenyon Review; L.A. Weekly; Left Curve; Lucky Magazine; Muleteeth; Northeast Journal; Nommo; ONTHEBUS; Pacific Association of Women Martial Artists Newsletter; The Black Scholar; The Jacaranda Review; Together Magazine; Roh Wedder; Snake Skin; Zyzzyva.

Deep appreciation for the people & institutions that have supported my vision:

Paul Vangelisti, Akilah Nayo Oliver, Sesshu Foster, Susan Carpendale, Christine Choi Ahmed, Ruben Martinez, Linda J. Albertano, Wanda Coleman, Beyond Baroque Literary Arts Center (Venice, California), Highways Performance Space (Santa Monica, California)

with special love for G. Colette Jackson

First edition, January 1994
ISBN 0-931122-75-9

Cover design by Pam Ward
Cover photograph by Susan Carpendale
Book design by Michael Reed
Typography by Prototype
Lost ancestor photograph from collection of the author

Completion of this manuscript was made possible by a literary arts grant from the National Endowment for the Arts, a federal agency.

West End Press • P.O. Box 27334 • Albuquerque, New Mexico 87125

Contents

.1.

Schwichtenberg
AZUSA & POMONA CAL.

History as Trash

White yuppies in santa monica go through their attics
     for stuff they will sell on side streets
25¢ for a photo of a colored gentleman in a high collar
     all bourgie & stiff & proper
     like he could read
a portrait rescued from the trash
     by my negro hands I hand picked
a picture of this brother
     shoulda been on his grandbaby's altar
     coulda been my uncle or
     my mother's teacher's preacher
somebody out there in the great
     gap-filled negroid space
in the fascinating stomach hurting trek of africans
     tearing up & building up
all the black energy wound up
right here on my ass
that same afro sticky history
all over the face of this man

photograph prove it

It's because he's a ghost
I think of death
& god & the god of dead negroes
& yo dead negroes bring to mind
spirits & the soul part smaller
than a breath & death again
the way all negroid bodies died:

     I believe he died angry
a hurt common to the colored at the time
     I believe he died mad
& his madness survives in the air of my world

He coulda been my people
good as the great grand grand momma I don't know
the lost ancestors screaming in my dreams
     & they don't got the good sense of an angel
     & they don't got the patience of a slave
     & they don't share no comforts, no secrets

In honor of the last ancestor
I hang my fists on nails
& sacrifice fried meat
because dead voodoo'n relatives
pick at the violence in my mouth
it's a sin & a shine they dizzy whispers
that crazed hiss lets me know
        death ain't silence
like the jesus clone promises
& the white god of santa monica
or the yuppie deities of indifference
need plenty closet space
& picks out what's useless
& trades it to strangers
for quarters, single bills
whatever they could get.

the voice of the rotten mother
booms like a ghetto blaster
the sound of the bad root
makes me hate music
i ask of the dope
i say to the smoke
can i get a hit
can i get hidden
from the room
where my mother's puking
is loudest, where her phlegm
& asthma medicine
her spotted face believes
i put out dirty
just like she said i was
bitch

i stay stoned
& flush it up w/ coffee
the flaps of my vagina sticky
it ain't like it was you
it ain't like it was something you
gotta remember
or go in the room
where she's slobbering spittle
where i suckled & split
it ain't like locks work on the mind
another bastard can't pick it open
never needle but constant weed
the voice of the bad root
kicks in curse words
the sound of the rotten mother
screams.

Child Molestation is a National Affair

In elementary school, the worn places
in my underwear were dirty secrets
under my skirt. But junior high issued me
a gym locker, a line to stand in, & a bench
cold & public where other girls
got their chance to snicker at my drawers.

The steam from the showers fogged my eyes
so I squinted at the pubic hairs of older girls,
I watched for their breasts, who knew
what a woman would grow to be, me in my
bra-less sore lumps, a bald vagina,
I seen my best friend Sheila bouncing
in the nude, I smelled her & saw
kotex underneath panty hose.

Sheila had matching pastel slips & clean brassieres.
Sheila had a father that bought her family money,
a brick house, a daily change of panties. Sheila could
curse, & she was moody, & wouldn't let her father
kiss her in the morning. At night he snuck in
her bed, wanted to get her ready for breaking
in, so he fingered her more & more.

Sheila could string together nasty words
like a ugly wino, a crazed washer woman sick
of her kids. Sheila showed me how to make
my fingers like a dick & balls that mean
      fuck you mother sucker
& Sheila pointed out the purple marks on girls'
thighs, the welts swollen in the steam,
exposed in hot water, w/ pointed breasts
& boxes of menstrual pads for feminine
protection, I didn't want no daddy,
would keep flat & dry forever
w/out a period of physical education:

keep tight my legs from sprouting
something a man might wanna touch
& keep my nasty panties, the holes
in my drawers, a private dirty secret.

Anti-Erotica

you have told me a lot of lies
you are not exactly like me
when your tough fingers pinch
the shape of the skin on your hands
remembers something like a tongue
a night stick

he was a short man inside my family
w/ big teeth & a hunting knife
(this is something i go through)
i am a girl
i am split in the middle
where the blood is painless
i take bad directions good
because a short man at a big family picnic
shrunk small as a snake & walked
in the hole. then he built a fire
& took out the knife he used to clean fish

my eyes are dead & open
i can hump but my head is turned backwards
the split was a juicy place
for your pushing/ i leave it open
for your use/   your happiness

he cut into my cave
this is something that takes me
this is fucked   up   inside
where i leave you alone
when you want it from the rear
i do it best when i leave
through the opening in my head
when i'm dead on my knees
pretending/   pleasing you i remember
he carved his name & left semen
that stinks & drips out slow

this is something i go through
this is first base
this first memory of arousal
touch my tittie & i'll bite
i spit
& dare you
to get hard.

Sex & the Mother Wound

1.
my clit as your hard candy/   my mouth's everywhere you want/
every opening slush/   like snow cones/   like i'll be your
bicycle/   i'll be nasty/   if you want/   i grew these titties/
i watched the black circle spread their weight/   do it like some
body bad/   somebody greedy/   we can hide under the dark/
or stake me in the open/

i have nothing inside
i have no name
i have nothing to remember
no thing to hate
fuck me
i have no name
my thinking shrinks up
i am smaller than the smallest pea
your eyes center the anchor
your thrust spills the drain
erase this nothing
everything black is yours
i have no thing to hate
i collapse on pulsing that hurts like love
dig into it
i have no self
i make you the god
an angel of vacancy

2.
the thing that hurts spills onto your palm
the thing that hurts fills in heavy of my ceiling
the thing hurting splits the clit like a razor
shape my mouth like a baby & crawl
i turn over the root of pussy
rear entry for a ride through fetal hell
the word of the sex god eats the mind like a parasite:
nasty
pussy
fuck
ooo shit baby
make me say jesus

the thing that hurts parts my lips w/ its memory
insert the spoon of raped babies
insert the hurt of infant girls fucked at home
the thing that hurts depletes its host
scoop out the origin of breath
my mother took a razor to the vaginal drama
a fester of puss linked to the rings
slice open & pour
the thing that hurts
penetrates the thing
that always hurts

3.
you are the big one
big one w/ hands
pull me out
screaming tear that breaks like morning sickness
pull my face out
fuck into this scar head
plant the seventeen seeds of beginning
home body
lit by tongue & slick
you are the one do me magic
body wailing
you lush
slush through me
sugar drives me into your blood
all things spiral around you so good
a home on fire w/ happiness

How to Love Monsters

1.
i always loved the werewolf
because he was so ugly
before the moon ever got full
he knew his sadness flipped
over into super bad attitude
his claws wet w/ the juicy
blood of his beloved

sounds like my mother
queen monster of my dream life
the flips she made after whiskey & late
night tee vee from numb
& quiet to bitch of the universe
her face full of curse words
her favorite extension cord
whipping welts on my back

i memorized her body language
& learned to love the wolfman
his need to confess
his prayers i pray
priest, police help me
old gypsy woman fix me
like a therapist calm me
down like dry herb
kill my nature, my dna
the blue prints in my blood
taken from a rotten mother
the monstrous interior copied
from a woman's scream

2.
last night i dreamt about a troll
w/ dead eyes & green skin
who easily spread his evil
w/ just a glance i pick up a metal weapon
& slice open his solar plexus
out of the bloodless wound

a vapor seeps & thickens
into another brother troll
who told me he tortures me
only because i deserve it
& i recognize him as my mother
as frankenstein & jaws
the universal bad guy monster
conjured to follow me through psychic changes
returning to the bad blood
xeroxed in a black childhood
rebirthed & living in nightmares
where i see him as sweet & hairy soulmate
all the monsters inside & out compressed
& i knew i would do what i always do:
love the monsters
hate the monsters
& then kill them.

Pets
karmic apology for lai lonnie

A hard xmas was the hardest
but sometimes/   one time/   we got a check fat enough to get
       even our pet a present: a doggie stocking w/ a plastic
       bone & chewy leather strips/   so happy we'd hug that dog
       that day we had a good xmas year/   we'd hug that dog &
       give her the toys & puppy yummies
that the dog wouldn't eat
& got left over
for us
when hard times made us laugh together in the kitchen/
       nothing but water or mayonnaise to eat/   I refused to
       eat dog food from the can, altogether too mushy for me
       to deal w/, but I think my younger brother did/   I think
       that's why he hates cats

Our momma was a soft woman/   really/   (sober)/   she could not
       not tell us no/   anytime some bitch down the street would
       give birth/   or a box in front of the liquor store/   we'd
       pull the babies out & beg our momma/   she all soft &
       smiling & saying yes/   so we'd go to books & the backs
       of our minds for extra ordinary pet names:
Mr. King Hound.   Smokey Josephine.   but I broke out w/ the
       most cool for Lai Lonnie/   cause I read in a play about
       an african prince/   lorraine hansberry gave me Lai Lonnie
       Asagai/   tough necked nigguh dog/   squat & mean/   I beat
       that dog
I took him to Berkeley/   he hated white hippies/   he got his
       leg broke in a fight w/ a german shepherd/   he bit white
       boys w/ beards/   but I beat his ass good whenever he
       fucked up/   I kept him in the student co-op w/ me &
       didn't nobody say nothing or else I could have called
       them racist:/   You just don't like black dogs!
White folks seemed to have just one family pure breed that
       was getting old & deaf & pissing on themselves by the
       time the kids went off to college/   one dog/   every
       summer/   every xmas/   they fed & re-fed that good old
       dog till the sucker died a clean death at the pound
We had seventeen dogs w/ no type/   just ghetto mutt mixes/
       most got hit by a car or died of distemper/   which was
       the worst.   the worst of the pet stories: death by

distemper & runny nose/   the yellow drip would turn green
& crust over/   we dug in the dirt & buried them in boxes/
a proud ritual of caring & crying & prayer/   but I never
learned/   another box of puppies & I was ready to beg
again

Pokey had a sweet nature & a wide toothy smile across a orange
& brown face/   he got the skin on his bad leg tore off/
snoozing under a car/   white folks would have called
daddy to warm up the station wagon to carry the pup to
the nice veterinarian/   I thought white folks lived in
a kind of absolute bliss cause they could always have
xmas/   & old, happy animals/   Beaver Cleaver & Lassie
made me sure/   while I carried bleeding Pokey in the
kitchen & asked my momma for some rags & she said
shit
the only rags i got is the rags i'm wearing
So I dealt w/ newspaper & brown paper bags & held Pokey's
muzzle w/ one hand & poured alcohol in the wound/   he
got better/   I figured I could be a dog doctor/   a
monkey nurse/   a healer to hamsters/   I liked to rub fur
& share my food w/ animals/   I hand fed Pokey & kept
him going w/ good conversation/   he got much better
but after that caught distemper
& died anyway

four gay guys from the beach
& white to boot
deliver pot to my door
i teach the younger to bless candles
because we are trying to convert him to paganism
he is a-political
he is w/out culture
but a pissed off feeling
can make him laugh anytime

'but am i being weird
am i showing off'
the second voice thinks
the one underneath the story
while the hands of the first voice
rolls another joint
'lotta power in these hands' i say
'we gone have to fight
cause you ain't got no politics
what do you think of the word fag?'

he is so young i had to forgive him
his stories so hard to come out
& i'm practicing being a man
so i yapped & yapped at him
explaining about fairies
the way radical homo boys
practice the craft alongside
local witches

he blinks & spaces
the good humored snooze possesses him
another cigarette, more bottled water
he don't like the word faggot but he uses it
two o'clock the candle burns down
the night runs out
my gay boys leave me
& i'm still lonely
i'm still mad

More Gods Means Less Slavery

It is the one god that I hate
the one lord of all mighty & minute
stuff that makes me mad
his sticky clouds/   his science fiction
his book locked in on law & punishment
would shrink me down
the big daddy god wants my anger small
& my knees collapsed

Yo pops/   I said once
this is a day unlike any other day
when such & such & such happened
& blip tee blam went down
& I'm bumming
I'm in need of a clue
what's my next move/   mister man
kneel down/   he told me
suck up your gut
& act like a god damn man
& after you die
things will be better

But things being hard as they was
I figured his penis was the problem
so I shaped the mud of his body
into a giggling girl/   just like me
& followed the goddess followers
into the caves of female comfort
where the goddess of everything substitutes big daddy
where her angels sing lullabyes
that bounce off the surface of the world
& leave the oil in the ocean
the mess in the city
the cracks in bitter children
for the law of karma to cope w/
you create your own reality/   the goddess answers
keep your personal cubbyhole clean

The goddess of one is into denial
so she piss me off too
cause she ain't hip to psychic death

16

the soul dies easier than the body
the spirit can be murdered
the good sense of teachers nuns & angels see nothing
just say no way/   they tell me
big shit/   I answer
tell it to my cavities
sing it to the violence choked in my mouth
promise me on halloween

So I let them both fall from the sky
gentle man & lady gods
I made them break apart
& every chip of holiness
is some kind of god I can use
cause when the one god broke
she/he expanded to include a bad
attitude & urban abuse

This is a poem about the triumph of shattered divinity
for example/   the god of orgasm sometimes makes an ugly face
the anti-god of time hangs out w/ the pseudo god of rent money
the first & last god I call on lives at the bottom of my gut
where bits of the smashed gods fell into me

If it weren't for the broken gods
I wouldn't have none.

Blood

He made fists when he stripped
& grunted blood into the head
to make the shadow of his penis huge
Bigger, bigger, best, he'd ask me
& I'd lie like every woman
lies still in bliss
& say Yes lover it was.

Honey it hurts
when you bite my tittie like that
I told him & he turned into the wall
& poured out cold sweat
& dreamt fear of the little dick dreams
fear of the missile cocked for hatred
And I'd turn momma
so he could turn baby
& whimper he'd never rape anyone
Not like in dreams, dreams aren't real
my dick's not too little, is it?

In the morning his blank face
ate my food like it was nothing
I caught him on the toilet staring down
at his ugly dead balloon he called it
my enemy, an enemy of women
And he went to bed too early or too late
all the blood stayed in his skull
all the seeds scared like abused children
& though it was no where near my time
I began to bleed.

Cats

What has crusted around your eyes
those tiny lines of lost moisture
like cream smeared on a slide
a sample of your wetness
taken by an impotent scientist
your softness lost in a statistic
about older, single women.

The fur on your cat
the purr from your pet
you know her habits too well
happily she hops on the bed
& you know just what it means:
she needs a scratch, some vigorous petting
& once rubbed, she's satisfied
she naps, curled like a baby boy
inside the void of your thighs.

You describe your last lover as vulgar
but sliding onto him was simple as drinking hot beer
he filled your gut & made you dizzy
the cat got lonely w/ you out so late
the cat got mad
& struck your open palm w/ exposed claws
& drew five thin lines of blood
so you'd remember never to leave her.

The odds are against you

remembering
you will earn five more wrinkles
at least an evil number of vulgar men
will pass through you again
& make the skin around your eyes
thin & ugly.

The Emergence of Barren Women

In the fifties my momma got caught
in the back of a musty pontiac
w/ her legs in a catholic koan
she wanted to do it & did
but got caught by a hard man
a missed period & me
soft bones & white spittle
me & my waste all over my momma's hands

As a child she dreamt of nursing
in white stockings w/ stiff cap
part of the colored elite rising in am. 1954
my mother the only colored speck
in st. teresa's school of nursing
first negress capped & pinned
after she finished nine months
she dropped out
when i dropped in her life

In the sixties i applied to berkeley
& got on the pill
the threat of hard men
shrunk w/ the tiny secret
i swallowed each morning
in college i buried my catholic roots
& studied biology, feminist archeology
dissecting the remains of old women
the details of their waste, their patience
i moved fast the morning after
my blood was late, cheap & quick
needles & scraping, let me out
the trap, a clot of black & red cells
that wanted to shit all over me
& make my dreams useless as a mother
in the nuclear age:

my mother sits
my mother remembers
a nursing cap flattened
in the back of my father's car.

Blood is a Bright Color & Tears are Clear
a poem in three voices

Ever get yourself square & situated
in a boxy apartment
cozy enough to ignore your neighbors
nice & nesty w/ a door that locks
in at least a couple of dead bolts
& some shit go down
& bust off a chunk of the world's funk
& smear it all in your living room
          I saw this lady shot through both legs
          the bullet lodged in her right knee
Somebody's massive chaotic mess
          I vaguely knew a woman bleeding
          on my carpet, her baby balanced
          on my hip. Her man, the fool
          w/ the gun & attitude enough to shoot
          He shot & ripped open my sleeping
Over to Isla Vista I rented
what I thought was a patch of peace
I had to move least two long bus rides
from over to where my momma stay
where the thugs & muggers
make the streets smell & fight
& folks so broke down
you got to pass them, walk past
they black eyes, the greasy
lines round they mouths
your heart can't pump hard
enough to help them
pocket ain't deep enough to share
          My lover called the paramedics
So you got to move
save your own ass
lock them double locks
& don't never crack the door
          I went into her screaming
          The baby girl never cried
          The mother convulsed
          The police brought guns & hunted down
          the man & took the child away

In a quiet neighborhood
where folk got jobs
& the shit broke loose anyway
It's like some living nasty
deep in the air, cruel & crusty
can float up & travel past
three or four bus lines & get you
& mess up your concentrated cool
your hard jobbing ass
& it ain't no reason
you never know why that cruelty is
living w/ you
breathing & bleeding in your living room

*　*　*

That night I smoothed the hair of my lover w/ my palms, w/ my fingers in his mouth, sleep was a numb dream spun w/ sharp, geometric shapes & dark, hard colors. And that first breath of the morning was cold as the harsh part of city living.

I wanted to see air, blue-ish & dead, I wanted to fly up, I needed to get out & make time act decent & be kind w/ me. But I went to work & I thought, 'I could tell them,' I could tell them, the story, how I got fresh blood from a married mother on my rug, & I called every bohemian I knew, & wrote seven-eight page letters, & told & re-told the shots ripping out my sleep, the doors of the neighbors shut or cracked, the vibration of the gun I take to bed w/ me, gripping my lover in abstract dreams.

And in the telling, that rush, that hot clarity of panic passed from me to my co-workers, my friends all got a piece of the violence & they shared w/ their children, their parents, this story about a couple that took in a woman shot through both legs, & the story passed inside the air of the words, the story passed in concentric circles of words of hurt, until the power closed down & stopped.

*　*　*

     Then my objective brain kicked in
So I'm talking
     & I got able to think
about the story
     what I'm telling you
about the hot bullet & blood
     about this baby
     w/ eyes so wide
     she couldn't cry

like I picked up her wound
& made it a scar of my own
                  So I'm gonna tell you
Gotta hold up this scar to the light

And let you see.

.2.

The Hundredth Boyfriend

On my way through an urban, straight-woman tradition
the promise I wanted lived & then died
I was bound to hook up w/ a man
so I slipped into a hollowed-out jazz solo
& followed sorrow up concrete steps
a moon split by a crack down the center
caught up w/ me

& again the 100th boyfriend
swept me into bizarre circumstances
the prince of cuddling & the demi-god of orgasm
got me into awkward positions
lifting laundry bags & popping blackheads

The boyfriend told a good joke
the boyfriend revealed a thousand secret troubles
hidden since adolescence
the boy's tight neck was constantly in need of a rub
his story soaked into my hands
my loneliness saturated w/ semen & red wine
I'm no loser, I say
my glands are busy w/ the work of love
I got me a man looks just like daddy

& again the 100th boyfriend hypnotized my vagina
while I memorized his best sport
he was as strong as two cappuccinos
his seed smoking w/ electricity
a liquid vitamin that aligned my spine
the hands of the 100th boyfriend
reached inside & massaged my heart
& got caught on a snag
& released a film of boyfriends
that got high in my head:

The 17th boyfriend had a hook dick
the 25th boyfriend liked the color purple & karl marx
the 37th boyfriend could fuck good & that's all
boyfriends 45, 72, & 67 were good as guns in a street situation
boyfriends 85 & 95 gave up beaucoup cash

I tell them all about the lunatics in the city
the maniac's silhouette that pops up in my skull
& the 17th boyfriend lost his erection
number 68 went home
the 99th met me halfway in the slime of our tripping
& kissed my fingers & rocked me

I tell the 100th boyfriend
I been through this before baby
I could be peppy & upbeat
w/ some juice & a little coaxing
I want a flag in the belly button of the 100th boyfriend
I want the shade of the shadow of the 100th boyfriend
to cool my hot ass down & stop the white noise of my mind
I aim to tattoo his memory bank
so when another number girlfriend comes along
he'll think of me when he fucks her
he'll always want me

But love is god & we know it
& god bugs out & messes up all the time
love cop a attitude & come up crazy
I snort it like cocaine
I pay too much for it
I act like it's cheap
I lost my habit & got stingy w/ the magic

But the 100 boyfriends were men that I loved.

How Boys Get Ruined by Growth

i had boyfriends before i had pubic hairs
nipples tiny as dimes
i wore glasses & wished for my period
james made me hot just by looking
i like his star trek/   his chess pieces
the night he read me leroi jones
his spit on closed mouth kisses sloppy
a spot to press even hotter/   i'd pull up my dress
i got a training bra the day we french kissed
we sucked mouths till our lips got numb
his tongue pointed like a fish & slimy
he never knew how slick my pussy got
flat chested/   practically a boy
james said/   body like a dude w/out muscles

he liked my mind/   he liked
physics & white folks' philosophy/   smart
nigger boy in the white man's school didn't have a chance
we knew it/   we knew our minds meant nothing
when we read baraka & soaked up coltrane
& sex was a dirty space we would break into
when my breasts caught up w/ his beard

he never promised
he opened up to me
the big V for still a virgin & sixteen years old

james left our talks/   to beat his meat
in a circle of horny boys
everybody aiming for the oreo in the middle
last one to come has to eat it
james told me my tits were too little
& went to beat his meat
so it got hard
& mean
& ugly.

the other girl was dumb
& got kept back in the eighth grade
her brain stupid enough to laugh at & hate
her tits pumped up w/ chemicals that said yes

she outgrew her training bra & had hairs & big legs
because she let him
he did it
james hustled to fuck the real thing
a nice nipple size
a tight nap in the pubic hair

a boy becomes a man by being hard
james found his erection enormous
& the other boys laughed
when he came last.

Dating the Dick Heads

One head takes me down to venice for foreign films
        w/ hot reputations & a cut-rate price. we suck
        natural popcorn in the dark, i let him crowd me
        into his arm pit, i let him touch me
        so he can feel lucky.

Another head takes me across town to restaurants in hollywood
        & orders stuffed chicken legs & lemonade made
        w/ artificial sweetener. the service
        of the third world servants pleases him
        they lift the legs w/ tongs & lay them on my plate
        'look sir' they say, 'she's smiling already.'

They call me, those heads, they feel me out, they pick up
        the check & whoosh open the door from the restaurants
        the door to the car, they say they don't wanna
        play games, they wanna be real, honesty
        makes the head harder
        i uncross my legs & put my palms on my knees.

What woman don't look good in restaurant lighting
        i paid cash for jafra foundation & white
        stick so i don't look so old
        my eye lashes glitter w/ technology & advanced
        yoga techniques hold back the sags.

He is wearing shaving lotion squeezed
        from the testicles of beavers.
        i am wearing robes that close
        at the neck & keep my shape
        a mystery.

Dessert is ordered & we talk:
        my ex-old man/ his current old lady
        boys & girls at war & how much of a feminist are you
        examples of bitches he has known
        you're over thirty & should probably think marriage
        putting the hump back into a doggish throw down
        & how not to intimidate men
        w/ stories of lesbian love
        race relations: black
        dick head asks if i prefer white

31

white dick head asks for the truth: is black dick head
bigger?

I am sweet i guarantee
& all i want is dinner.

Another Anti-Love Poem

When coffee is a dangerous treat
& hot women sleep off their ice cappuccinos
in the heat of a harlem summer
then these jitters will force me out of bed
force me to open the door that lets you in
& lets that cold public air
crawl up my legs & surround me

Beware the thick thighs of black
intellectuals who lift weights
beware the laughter of the colored bourgeoisie
I remember white drops of semen
absorbed by my uterus
I remember fussing & scolding
& negroes all in my shit
& I was almost sucked in again
almost eaten
almost another 'nother alligator nigguh
tasting my tongue & trouble
sliding into me

You flip like the fish of the surrealists
& I know your ways
you protect like a bull, bond like a kitten
& no one understands you
you carry rope, matches & scotch tape
you are connected
& people will talk
but not about me
besides solitude
my closest partner is fear
could you wrestle that bastard to the ground
tie me up, light a fire & scotch tape my wounds?

No. read my lips.
fuck you. go home.

i'm dating black intelligence
so i don't need no dog pose/
                          yo baby
the brutal home boys called him punk
what could any small man do
any man w/ a fat heart muscle & bi-focals
do but collect weapons
& sing hard songs to his motorcycle
my weapon is a dog pose/
                          yo baby
cut off anything from below the head
i'm thinking he's so smart
he could seduce me from women
& the thrill of tying up white boys
a solitary brother w/ high-tech musical instruments
& a gumby on his key chain/
                          yo baby
you ain't got no breasts i know
& the tension in your cock
is not like a pistol at all
not like the juicy battlefield
where love is repellent & reminder
can't nobody hang
nobody loves & gets away w/ it
i'm thinking can you feel it
intellectual nigguh man
w/ your wire rims & long sentences/
                          yo baby
this is a celebration of piercing insights
& a cool sleep black enough
to make me forget everything
& make you
super fine negro boy
stop thinking.

The Price of the Ride

My open throat drowns
on a black nipple
while my spine curls
like the fist of an infant
in the dark womb
baby

I am a knife
prone to castration
& you are fruit. Sometimes
a cute nut laughing
or a mother wiping
the sleep from my eyes:
                                    No good
because of the scary jail
the cell padded for me
when my mind goes blank
thinking of you.
Sin. Trouble. Suffering
another lie I tell myself
about what goes inside
what assaults & insults carved in my cave
by men. The world would flush me away
& squeeze my heart in a cage
& blink w/ or w/out hatred
if I loved you.

Pretend you are my roommate.
Pretend you are a cousin from Texas
in need of a nap & my bed is the only place.
Pretend you are all man but
w/out a penis or hard attitude

Miss Butch Lady
the evil bulldagger found me in a closet
& finger fucked me silly
in exchange for sugar
or acid
or apples
because I went w/out breakfast.
The birth mother neglected me
that's why I need you.

What are men
but the missing piece of power
I bend down for.
All love is humiliation
every opening pushed through
like a scab
a dried booger peeled off
to expose the primal lack of courage
to take your hand
to place your vagina in my mouth.

The price of the ride
is another layer of lies
another mask of sorrow
pasted on the face of a woman
I cannot love.

2 Black-Skinned Love Losers Reconsider Gertrude Stein

I. Portrait of You Inside of Me

many of you think we.
many of you be thinking we which means me & you plus other
      miscellaneous people.
many of you be thinking we which means me & you plus other
      miscellaneous people who think like we do.
      like the way we think.
      like the way we think & deal & process consciousness like
      we do.

and in this way that we think, we think emotion is very important.

that emotion is very important to those of us who think about emotion
      in this way.
that feeling & thinking both are important to our process of
      consciousness.
that the way we process & deal w/ our feelings & thinking makes us
      a conscious we.

which indeed is a we.
which indeed is a we that be constantly thinking & looking &
      understanding our process of consciousness in this way.

which indeed is a comfort & companionship & community & we like
      it.

II. Portrait of the Other

& so some of you think why.
and so some of you think why many things but this time about love.
and so some of you think why someone to love who does not process
      consciousness like we do.
      in the way we do.
why somebody who is outside the we of our consciousness who
      does not process consciousness in the way that we do.

and so there was a lover who did not process consciousness about
      feelings & thoughts in the way that we do.

and so there was a lover of extreme sexual honesty & loveliness &
      fat lusciousness who was a lover who did not process

consciousness like we do.
and so there was a lover living inside the very space of me who was
     not like the we that we are.
a lover who lived as bone & blood inside the very space of me,
     inside the very space of me that loves to process
     consciousness w/ you in this way.
and so there was a lover living & breathing & giving orgasms to the
     me who belongs to the we of you.

and so the power of loneliness became a great power.
and so the power of loneliness got strong & fat & selfish.

III. Dialogue

what i'm trying to say is that it's hard to say what i'm trying to
say

     you ain't said shit

i'm trying to say that there is something i need to say that is
hard to say

     you ain't said shit about nothing

i'm trying to talk about the feelings that are involved in talking
when i try to talk to you about what is so hard for me to say

     you ain't said shit about nothing
     except talking about talking which ain't saying shit
     because you ain't said shit in the first place

i'm trying to say that it is hard to say what i have to say when
i feel like you can't understand what i am saying about what i have
to say to you. plus other things

     things like what

things like a hardness to the barrier that keeps me away from a
sense of you & feeling like i can say what is so hard to say to you

IV. Self-Portrait

there is the power of the lover who gives orgasm.
there is the power of the lover who gives orgasm that has a power.
there is a power of the orgasm that has the power to wash over the
     stickiness of the day and the ugliness of the night.

there is the power of the orgasm that widens me.

there is the power of the lover who gives orgasms that widens &
   soothes the me of the we that processes consciousness in the
   way that we do.

there is the power of the way we process consciousness in the way
   that we do.

there is the argument of emotion & thinking that seeks resolution
      in the way we process our consciousness in the way that we do.
      there is the emotion that beats up thought.
      there is the body which beats up thought.
                there is the thought that desires power over the
body. there is the thought that desires power over the body.
there is the thought that desires power over the body.

there is the lover who comes w/ the power of the love based erotica & the
power of orgasm that washes the stickiness of the day & ugliness of the
night & warm heartbeat like an infant who rocks w/ no consciousness.

Politics of the Bisexual Deep Fry

i said
    my woman left me
    & i don't think i'll ever have another girlfriend
she said
    i must have my mouth on you

i said
    i'm not attracted to white women
she said
    i like the darkness of your nipples

i said
    it's not exactly because of inherent ugliness on white skin

    it's because white girls always think i'm a butch
    you're so strong they say
    & bat their eyelashes
    which makes me feel like feeding my cat to my dog
    you're so powerful which of course means male
    you're so tough inside that rough black skin they say
    black skin which means black attitude
    which of course means mannish
she said
    you're such a girl

i said
    plus lesbians hate bisexuals
    bisexuals are the nigger of the queer community
she said
    all my ex-lovers are bisexuals

i said
    even though my family kicked me out
    & black nationalists say my kind destroys the black family
    even though a queer is a queer is a queer
    to any christian homophobe
    i know you hate me

    i know you can't hear inside my private story
    you think my addiction is for dick
        & i want to hide behind the shadow of a man

i don't want a bisexual movement
i don't want a bisexual newsletter rap group parade
i don't want to steal or pollute the purity of lesbian space

i want you to care about me inside my private parts
i want you to let me be the queer that i am
& know i am not your enemy

plus i'd like to get laid

she said
maybe we can work something out

i said
plus lesbians run out of energy so quick
lesbian bed death

i've heard stories of 3 & 4 year celibate relationships
lovers who turn into sisters
passion dies w/ time
girls don't really have a sex drive
drive as in driven as in need as in got to have some

i've seen those feminist videos
soft vanilla sex
nobody sweats
nobody fucks
nobody gets nasty
rumor has it
feminists don't like to fuck because it makes them too
vulnerable

beware the single-celled lesbian woman
who knows the body language of cats
who can take care of exactly herself
who knows exactly what her self
    alone in a room wants
who doesn't wanna be opened by fire
who doesn't wanna fuck or possess or control

her orgasms are the strokes of baby fingers
that aim to imitate masturbation

she will not give it up to you
she won't let herself want it

she said
i got something for you

this has no ego mode
this has no sperm
this is a toy for like-minded women
who wanna take that plane of infinite pleasure

i said
maybe we could work something out

Don't Wanna Lose Your Love

one time i was gliding
on the 101 downtown
after the rain & the lights
were lit & the city was
orange & black from the night
& the buildings were
tall rectangles centered
in the black crack of the world
in front of me & the orange
seemed magic
seemed like my madness
was making the color cool
making the color promise
that the poison-us grit
& burned-out bad attitude
frozen in the physics of l.a.
could do me no harm

i don't wanna lose
the long rides that do me
good as drugs sometimes
& you & love & lies & youth
aren't things i can hold on to
but this city
her nasty oils
when the sky cries water colors
this metal bubble of silence
where no one looks me in the eye
sugar, this shit is lasting.

.3.

daughters wait for the wounded to scream themselves
to death
daughters choosin to be women
lick their wounds with their own spit

til they heal

—Ntozake Shange

Options for Girls: Patience & Loathing

once there was a girl. once there was the birth of a girl who dropped out of a stressed-out uterus, dropped into a freaked-out time when all the blood in the universe was stressed. all cultural memory swore to her cavemen are demi-gods, warfare is natural & prostitution was our first work. recorded mythologies ordered her to hang in the sky & reflect, like a stupid moon. once there was a girl who grew smaller than her bones, softer than her muscles, who learned no older women had glory, who learned to clip off parts of her body of knowledge. to attract someone. to have something to do. beauty aggressed her, the family colonized her, & the good way & the bad way broke open her only choices: women w/ patience & women w/ hate.

the woman who waits feels no power surge when the bloods come. she
      consumes lemon-flavored daisy douche & uses her
      open, slick under parts as meat clamps. her things
      are predictable: pressed sheets, de-clawed animals, &
      crossed thighs.
a cookie cut from a media imprint, she commits her soul to her lover.
      she duplicates her self w/ a split labia & poo poo diapers.
see her small. see her last when you are the most tired. come to her
      compromised by confessions, ready for baby food. the
      woman who waits reminds us of nobody important.
      another woman w/ no political strategy, no warrior voice.
the woman who waits puts her hair up & denies threats. she shrinks,
      she hides, she walks into trouble like a poodle raised in
      a cage. the woman who waits learned nothing from her
      rape experience except the same old mouth full.

           men find hate for the woman who waits/ men make liquid aggression that explodes from their dicks/ law man & jesus man & knife man entertain movies of her terror/ bitch word for the woman who waits/ kitchen knives for the clit of the woman who waits/ battered as the white sky/ bruised as clumps of terrorized blood rushes to the wound of the woman who waits/ whistles & mace & house keys lock her into fear/ just wait & all hurt drains from you. faith as numb hands folded, proper, first, last & always, she waits.

the woman who hates is not her sister.
the woman who hates likes to be naked; she recognizes her nipples as
        arsenal, her smell as weaponry, everything red or round
        inside her body as stockpile.
last-minute fun girl, always ready to perk, the woman who hates laughs
        like the fire of trouble, the joy of the woman who
        hates melts into high-cholesterol stomach-heavy feasts
        of sensation. somebody wishes they could eat her.
        somebody wants her mascara to run.
see her like this: orgasm as black & cool & home to her meanest sorrow.
        bathed & seasoned & freshest in the center of the night.
        she storms & steams & pulls on your aura.
the woman who hates hates in particular her mother, all neat baby-craving
        cunts. cut her w/ the promise of mommy-ness. puncture
        her w/ children as the best workshop. on mother's day
        she worships her tampons. on father's day she psychs
        up for the hunt.
her downfall is wrinkles in the neck, makeup grease balls, & the day a
        saggy ass & titties like socks takes her. you old woman.
        you old ugly-ass childless woman. men shriek at her &
        fuck her anyway.

        men find hate for the woman who hates/ men make liquid aggression that explode from their dicks/ law man & jesus man & knife man entertain movies of her terror/ bitch word for the woman who hates/ kitchen knives for the clit of the woman who hates/ battered as the white sky/ bruised as clumps of terrorized blood rushes to the wound of the woman who hates/ whistles & mace & house keys lock her into fear/ she excels in the feminine circle of ass-eating snake. hatred as beginning that obscures sources of faith, first, last & always, she hates.

and
once again
as always
in the beginning

there was a girl. a girl who could not swallow the shut-down images served w/ her eggs. once a girl heard her world whisper: your traditions are traitors/ trust no one. once a girl who turned away from the mother of her body, the guilt of the momma of her people, wishing she didn't have to hurt them. once a girl closed her palms around the nucleus of silence, made a fist around the elements of emptiness & yanked her self out. once a girl sanded down the mask, peeled away denial, & inhaled the air of solitary wonder. once a girl had sex w/ truth. once a girl did the nasty w/ righteousness. once there was a girl, just a girl, who screamed from the top of a flight of stairs I GOT MY PERIOD & knew it was truly an excellent thing.

Womanist Face Aches

—dedicated to Keith Antar Mason & the Hittite Empire

history ain't none of my friend
     history loud talks me like a worn out worker
     a cleaning lady w/ humiliations
     hidden in the folds of her skin
culture warns me to hush my mouth
     & honor the blood lines
as in brother/   as in black/   as in kin ship of slavery
     the way i can't razor cut the women & men apart
     the afra/   afro/   american chained
     shackle of nigger sensibilities:

          yesterday i drove past 4 black youth
          handcuffed & on their knees
          across the street from usc
          & like 'why-did-they-need-6-cop-cars-
          for-4-boys-in-tennis-shoes' type thing
          & every time rashidi visits the west side
          he gets stopped
          & hassled & searched

          never happens to me

          & antar told me he can't walk up on
          a white woman alone at the insta teller
          cause his shiny face & hair bumps
          just about stop her heart
          dead from beating

          & i usta wanna be a man
          but not for the dick part
          if i could just play off
          a couple extra inches
          & draw a bogus moustache w/ a felt tip pen
          i could roam venice beach in peace

          except as a black one/   i'd look criminal
          w/ shoulders & penis & animal instincts
          cause the man to track me down

just like history hunts my tongue
     w/ its grotesque evidence
     traces of coon
hunts klansmen took for sport

celebrating white supremacy w/ razor cuts through the groin
& stuffed our brother's open mouth w/ his own testicles

    mother/   sister/   baby
love cut the body down
    & cleared the breathing passages
    & cleaned the corpse as if it were a premature infant
precious & bound for better times
sweeter places in the future tense
    when manhood could recover & recycle

history/   as in story/   as in stolen/   whipped & lied to
culture as in colored/   as in strips of the dissected heart
what does a survivor of the jewish holocaust say
    to the remains of an african one:
            i know you
your center soft as domesticated animals
wronged as the white rats who absorb human cancers
my vagina the most dangerous thing i own
    sends out an aura of infinite vulnerability
    & wraps me in skin
    linked to the suffering

i stretch for body parts that won't go numb
    bring this heart out of shock
    re-birth the dark pulse
a marrow of gut emotion
    black enough
    to swallow & digest this
the twisted present
tense.

Traditional Post-Modern Neo-HooDoo Afra-Centric Sister in a Purple Head Rag Mourning Death and Cooking

1.
Traditional:
>   that mean has a voice & a person
>   you can relate to
>   & probably a plot w/ a beginning, middle & end
>   & if you don't understand it, the poem don't work

Post-Modern:
>   is because of 1945 when the americans dropped
>   the first nuclear bomb
>   on nagasaki asia
>   & got everybody thinking about death of the species
>   more problems, more paranoia

Neo-HooDoo:
>   1972, *Conjure*, by Ishmael Reed
>   deals out of a black bohemian mentality
>   also post-nationalist BoHo Nats of new york city

Neo-HooDoo:
>   sound a lot like voodoo
>   also new, which is not real

Afra-Centric:
>   afra-centric
>   like first colored was the compliment
>   then negro was the compliment
>   & nigguh was always the insult
>   then change happened
>   & black was everything beautiful
>   & africa was new
>   then nigguh was the precious secret
>   then afro-mantic
>   now everything
>   now afra-centric
>   now of course news of the first mother of the first womb
>   in the first cave of afra-centric
>   africa

Afra-Centric:
>   coined by Asungi, womanist artist

Sister:
>   this means of a woman
>   of the uterus root

In A Purple Head Rag:
Purple:
    a color
    a color like colored like
    nigguh was so black he was blue
    girl was so blue she was purple
    the color purple
    which is Alice Walker which is our time
A Head Rag:
    this is a head rag
    as relaxed
    as home
    as natural
Mourning Death:
Morning:
    as the sound of the first day
Mourning:
    as the sound of hurting for the loss of a dead person
Death:
    as barrier to the spirits
And Cooking:
    as sexual energy
    as communal response
    as human feeling

2.
Morning was the softest hum
an anti-music buzz that ached
in my face when he died
a white boy suicide
in love w/ the evil in elvis
& conjured a heart attack
w/ cigarettes & despair

All the hard & good people
who loved him at a funeral
party freak out

I was about to call
I was ready to wail
        ready to grieve & receive
the basic wisdom to deal w/ the situation
I was trying to be connected
to the black at the bottom of my genes
bad enough to box w/ grief
that plus some impulse to take
care of business & feed people
to taste & stir & season
& pass out plates solid w/ material radiance

It's me thinking
cooking is sometimes a contradiction
folks w/ european privilege
people w/ penis privilege
get happy on the service
& greedy w/ my love
I won't be nobody's mammy
but at a wake when folks mourning
when common & good sense both take a whipping
when understanding sits down, trembles & falls into fits
it's a sin not to cook
it's a sin to hold back any kinda magic you got going

It's me thinking
I gotta come across
so I put an honest drain on my mystery
I cooked
I tried to look good
I ate & danced w/ strangers
I listened for the echo that the dead heart leaves
& wore the color purple

54

It's me remembering
trying to sing
that plus holding myself
I had to soothe & quiet somebody
& ended up witness
to this pain washing through
a body of people
who came together
because he left us
because he had to
do what all bodies have to do
sometime

which is pass on
let go
& finally say good bye.

Cubist Poem: Momma Read It Right

i say
i mean
girlfriend
   momma read it right
   that's a whole day's cooking

 i mean the pot ain't got no problem
 & the attitude come from somewhere

    you always got to notice
    who's eating
    who's not eating
show me some kinda respect
 just be real w/ me
   don't be putting money in your mouth

    girl can fuss
   she ain't beating this drum for nothing
    seem like she was beating it w/ her heart flesh
them blood line wounds
they follow you
   it's a sin to hold back
   any kinda magic you got going

the pendulum is about to stop
you best hope the point
don't be on you

Uterus Root

"this class i took in santa cruz
in women's studies
was my first real woman-identified experience
my first long straight look
at the big & wonderful & historically relevant
vagina, the pussy, the mother cunt
& how every body comes through the womb
& how the white boy existentialists
a dying breed, say:
you are born alone
& we know better
we know your momma was right there
right from between her legs
your first home
the sound of your first heart beat
set your ass up for the drum
& dancing & fucking & everything that is a natural rhythm

it was the feminists first
hipped me to the root
the uterus root
see boys make their seed
they just mix it up on a regular basis
on a day-to-day basis
on a minute-to-minute basis
& discharge it
their bodies expel those seeds
into the indifferent night
nocturnal ejaculation
when they can't find nothing to catch that nut

for them straight girls
& they boyfriends
honey, he's probably fixing some up
right now, something hot & sweet
he wants to let loose in you
someplace, tonight

but girls see
we was born w/ every egg we'll ever have
we made every one while we was growing

inside the womb of the mother
so my momma made the first molecule of me
inside the belly of the grandmother
& the grandmother held the first biochemical trace
of my ass & passed me
inside the belly of my mother
& my mother walked around close to twenty years
w/ me inside her ovaries
& she guarded me against venereal disease
& technology
& i set up there inside her
w/ all the other eggs
floating in the blood of her emotion
& the father came along & touched her
& i commenced to grow"

Kwanza Card for Paris & Rashidi

happy kwanza
know thyself
eat til you grease
amani means peace
natty dread makes for funky american lingo
the aryans invaded from the north
archeology, evolution & prayer
now/ deal w/ that

happy kwanza
twelve twenty six to one two new year
i want to have a secret w/ you
i win/ you win
beyond biology
but do you like potato pie
do you want green xmas pajamas
first thing my daddy
eat the new year
is pink pig feet meat
eat til you grease
go on & knock it out

happy kwanza
seven days & seven principles
the egyptian creed for women of the holy order
know thyself
kissed by an african scholar
tongue kissed in the shade
of a winter palm tree
i been doing pretty good myself
going round the sun
the sky busted loose
in a black theme boomerang

happy kwanza
i pour my emotion into the world
you are entering my life
now/ happy kwanza
deal w/ that

Translate This Fuck Face

It was this nigguh run up on this euro-am.

& this euro-am. said: 'you know you can't talk to me because your language is a dialect of english'
& the nigguh said: 'you know i can't say nothing to you because you can't understand me because you won't listen because you think my language is a dialect of english'

& this euro-am. said: 'you know i don't know what you saying because i don't understand it because i never heard it before because you got that mutant dialect going on because you probably ain't making no sense no way'
& the nigguh said: 'say you & me was talking. say we was talking about something. say i say me say you you was talking about something, saying we could talk. say you in me i could could talk & understand you & then we talked because we we could talk, we you understood the dialects of english & the roots of europe caught in an african beat'
& this euro-am. said: 'if you process your language some, put your rhythm in a dictionary, make that sound inside a euro cerebro encyclopedia, yo, i could hang. i could deal & hang & rap in a dialect of listening english'
& this euro-am. listened for the translation
& this euro-am. thought she heard the nigguh say:

quote i put my language in a box called translate to english

but this is not what the nigguh said

& the nigguh said: 'you know i can't say nothing to you because you don't listen to me because you think you can't understand me because you believe my sound is an off color slur of primitive beats, a tangent to the center of the west, you know, my language won't work into you because of an arrogant distance in the realm of your mind, you know'

& this euro-am. said: 'say what?'
& the nigguh said: 'nothing'
& this euro-am. said: 'that's what i thought you said'

& the nigguh said: 'hmmm.'

Guidelines for Brothers: How to Heal Rape

Sister-love, Auntie Mae, yo big momma
dear been took down, gagged & broke into
understand brother man
a sick spurt sours her vagina
splinters her love-fuck connection
splits our
do-it-to-me instinct
our widening
of eager thighs
for you.

We could say
community got a problem
a dead white man's thing
messed over our mother africa
mutating new born black sons
till we just don't know how to act
an easy passing of the buck
to the honky. Protecting of the buck's
violent member
ship in the international patriarchy
bent on hating women.
We expect more of you, we need more.

Listen. One half of black women
jolts up from dread sleep
& dream of the colorless rapist
seeds of disease spattered on our face.
We need a final peace
to close the wound & re-open the body
male spirits w/ eyes
as open to the terror as ours
thick w/ tenderness & patience:

Wish peace for women.
& keep our dick soft
while you wanna listen
& accept her hurt & hate
a god damned dog did this
separating thing, don't never

get it up & in
when you got a gut of hate
from this white man's world

Let the love
you pass to her
be pure.

Why I Hate Music
(for & against a blues aesthetic)

I wanna talk bad about you
I wanna confiscate your comforter
strip off your party noise
& force the remains of a semi-conquered race
into the soft center of your ears

I wanna dissect your demi-gods
those media drunk heroes & she-rose
their pedicured fine-ness
their lame tame lyrics
that xerox & recycle
the tickle of romantic love
like all we got to do
(in this life) (in this world)
& fuck the fuckable
& endure the breaks

inside the music is a history we betray
inside the saxophone is a trace of holocaust wisdom
lesson burned into underclass
skin we go dumb to

pay attention: black
ass slaves distilled
the hurt of humiliation
into a musical code
the nouveau negro jesus
partied in christian tents
& hallucinated grace
that mutated into jazz
& transfigured the negritude
blues into white metal rock & rap
& here we are
in the wake of neo-upper class
colored entertainers
who do benefits for african famines
who do charity for burnt-out farmers
here we are w/ ex-ghetto brothers
rapping & lounging &
lusting their zillion dollar homes

once fame invades their body space
they swell up like a greedy penis
& hire mexicans to cut their weeds
they do interviews
they give intimacy to air brushed photos
& admit/ they knew it/ they were special
from the start.   you eat
their trance like a tranquilizer

I hate you because you're happy
because a cd & heavy-duty speakers
erase your genetic grief
because a rhythm & wordless melody
pacifies you like a common beast
you are soothed
you are cooled
& your numbers
are enormous.

Tantrum Girl Responds to Death

COOKIE
cookie was hard the way women can only be hard/ not street or drug
tough but more like that roughness certain women steal/ thieves of
male power/ shirts & short hair cuts/ w/ musculature molded from
the men's camp/ & a stride w/ all the power of an honest erection/ but
w/out the greed

MY THING
i keep my hair long for lesbian get togethers/ i always wear skirts &
bangles/ my wish is for the mannish type to wish their yang into my
yin/ cookie had serious flirt going on/ not my type for the steady
thing/ cookie: you ain't nobody to talk to so why trip because you died

CANCER
from lumps of stress lodged in her breasts/ shrunk in a hospital room
while chicken shit members of her family shunned their bulldagger
daughter/ son wouldn't call/ & all the queer christians took turns
driving out to cucamonga/ gay people death vigil & the hot wire phone
tree w/ news of her weight loss/ cookie, big chested, greedy eater at
our card parties, shriveled down to bones & a nonsense daze sinking
in her eye sockets

KADDISH
it's happening/ it's happening/ like a virus of the boys got confused
& stole a body in our camp/ it's happening that fat cookie is dying/
big, lusty, bull dyke cookie is coming down/ breaking down/ making
ruins of her body/ the dark of her eyes detach/ needles & tubes sound
ugly mantras & stink/ all spirit crushed by collapsing organs/ all soul
silent/ & traceless

SO WHAT
she didn't know me/ i winked at her/ i dragged her into my
masturbation fantasies/ i tried to lift my skirt & wave the vanilla
scent i use to lure butch gay girls/ sex & death is dancing/ death
who can't get me like people w/ root love/ fear of death who leaves
me when i'm bored/ when i'm arrogant

FUNERAL HOME
a cave of refrigeration/ the chest of the undertaker sunk in the center/
his eyes have no history/ his mouth no natural heat/ numbers in
his mind like i get off at 7/ it's tuesday/ twelfth funeral this week/
thirty two hundred dollars/ room #5/ services at 8/ caskets in cells
w/ low ceilings/ cells w/ sticky dust

65

VISION

i am on guard for perversion/ i am hunting the lessons of death/ the excrement of love liars/ i don't give a care except to watch you/ i'm sorry i never got you in bed/ death presses at my temples/ i am ready to rebel/ i will never have children/ i shiver like death needs a tantrum/ a cheerleader/ a lesbian lover screamer girl

PEARLS

cookie has on pearls w/ rosy rouge/ cookie has puffed out hair & bad taste secretary's bow tie/ cookie looks like somebody's auntie, who had parakeets & ate biscuits/ her body a complex lie of femininity/ the closet of a casket/ her pearls the polished bones of fish enslaved by men

DEAD MEETING OF THE FAMILY

all her blood relatives dressed in black & shine/ marched in from the void they left in the cancer ward & took up the front rows of the home/ her son who called her freakish/ her nana who cursed her sinful mouth/ her mom who beat her through her boyish adolescence/ gripped hands & slung snot/ faggots & lesbians who saw death empty her face/ cornered/ crowded in the row in the back

VISION EXPLOSION

i talk to my fingers/ touch her, i say/ this is your chance/ will she feel like furniture/ death in the flesh w/ no real reason to mourn/ & sorrow ropes my throat/ you ain't no femme, i tell cookie/ you wasn't no frustrated straight girl i scream/ you was a natural bulldagger/ a lesbian ass woman/ i ain't lying just cause you dead/ cause your momma wanna front the betrayal off/ & by then they are on to me/ & they pull me back into line

TANTRUM GIRL RESPONDS TO DEATH

i swallow the lesson like pills from a wealthy doctor/ i ingest the family tribute like more proof against blood bonding/ & i calm down off the death addiction/ just in case death has a parasite clause/ don't want this shit sticking to me/ don't wanna pay for arrogance in the death of some beloved/ death could come around & kick my ass good

The Craft

To write, you gotta get your head full of yourself
& you gotta divorce all the falseness of the world
        from your brain molecules
you gotta feel like god
        as important as the crutch god
        the trickster god
        the god of laughter & puns

To write you gotta
        swell up your chest
        blow out your heart & empty your veins
of blood that might bleed if you cut yourself in the kitchen
        you gotta think your stuff is stiff w/ iron
        your spirit the center of the world
 your hands the connective tissue of all the type
        writers that ever put out a chapbook
you gotta ego-rush, chest-thump & finger-fuck
        yourself into literary orgasm, alone
w/ no feedback at
all, alone.

It is better than sex or human understanding.
It is beyond & into the amazing pool of the cultures
of the world compressed. It is cool.
It is putting yourself into the cool-est cool club
in the universe. It is separation from the mundane & union
w/ the divine: it is live.

        Then you fart, or break
your toe, or fall
        into a rash of childhood memories
        that want the blindness of self pity
then some slim gives you a hard time
        on the streets
& all that swirling power comes
        back, flat, into your plain black
        hands & thin skeleton
that will soon bend w/ age & death.

To write, you gotta gag on blood
        gag on broken bones
you gotta court & marry the scum of organized life

the indifference of our mother earth
who wounds & rots & eats unlucky children
you gotta cross the big street
dodge the big cars
get hit
get hurt
get mad
& write about that
you gotta limp, be ugly
be smelly & full
of the funk stuck to your hands.

It is meaner than lust,
harder than human relationship.
It is lonely as adolescence for a zit-faced girl.
It will absorb & exhaust your spirit of fire & open eyes.
It is separation from the mundane & union w/ the divine:

It is live.

Sensei Maria's Story

"i was born small
because i was born early
the experts said i would die early too
& when they watched me crawl
they gave up on my legs
& said i'd never take the steps i take now
now i throw side kicks
now i see my limbs fighting
now i feel my knees & remember the braces
that buckled at the top of the thigh
a first & last resort for premature infants
iron braces held together w/ leather straps
for the toddler i was
for more than a year
i unbuckled & sat
i buckled & walked
i unbuckled & sometimes i would fall
like all children fall down
in public & the people pulled back
like i was ugly
too horrible to help
too strange to pick up
a baby crying inside heavy braces
like they might catch it
contagious metal contraptions
infectious disability
the horror on the faces of strangers
before i walked w/out braces

now my legs serve me inside okinawan kata
now the hurt in my memories serves me
when i serve karate
i work self-defense technique
w/ women in wheelchairs & men w/ prosthetics
when blind women spar
the deaf women fill the dojo w/ kiais
we seek perfection in training
the power of karate for everyone
anyone w/ or w/out braces
inside our circle of beauty & power
so no one is left
fallen & locked out again."

Poem in Gratitude for San Kyu

o sensei of everything

sensei of the disabled stars & the battered ozone
sensei of the cruel street & dirty concrete details of my living
sensei of the blockage
     of the beauty
     of the blackness
     in the night
    the urban dark that gives
    no peace to women
sensei of the mysogynist creation myths
    the erect gods of punishment & frozen emotion
    the histories written to break the will of pickaninnies & sluts
    & every color cunt bitches

    when the race war calls on me
to act a fool
    when the dragon baby throws a tantrum
because the rotten mother is drunk again
    when rage & payback call on me
to damage human flesh
i call on you
o
sensei of the x-ray vision & tuned up intuition
o symbolic sensei
    who knows all things
    accepts all things
    believes all things
there is a splinter
there is a crack
there is a wall
the sky split & spit me to the ground
    like a turd
    like animal waste mixed in blood
    refusing to clot
my name a streak of wounds too stubborn to heal
o sensei of the screwed up universe
    of children pounded into perverse shapes & penetrated w/ hate
o sensei
o sensei

o sensei of the burned out wish for quiet
        of the desire for peace
        that honors the disease of its roots
o sensei of the black meditation
        of the warm breathing space
        the colorless place between the in & exhale
sensei of the natural forces
        meant to free us

this balance inside my fists
this belly as smart as my brains
these toes in line w/ moving target
i shake my hidden fist at bad guys
i cut paths around crazies & let them have their wretched space
i gather up girls
        w/ knobby knees & ugly glasses
        & promise them
like i was never promised
        you can make from the mud of your suffering
        you can cut a path of power from the arc of your breath
        you can find your feet as holy instruments
a link to the girl hero in the earth
so delicate
so solid
that the spark
& truth of your survival
will follow you
all your days.

definition of japanese words in text:
san kyu: the rank of brown belt
o sensei: the highest ranking instructor (she/he that passes knowledge
        of power, balance & morality in self-defense)

The Loneliness of Healing

it comes to you like a grainy dream: you feel only your head, floating eyes & a chain of words until an axe woke up nerves in the spine. the doctor sends you to a neurologist who sends you to an orthopedic surgeon who sends you to a chiropractor who bursts your budget & swears it's emotional, it's stress related, it's bad ideas bouncing around in your insides. you were hoping for a pill, some greek-named disease, rare but easily cured, w/ a prescription poured into your palm from an opaque bottle. fix me you say, i am loyal as an automobile, quiet as a girl child. i can't exercise, i can't carry my baby, i can't go to the bathroom, i'll lose my job. crying flusters doctors but proves their point. you'll have to bite your new age hate & hire a therapist.

one night sleep wanders away from you, the household snoring, you slide like a ghost, & make yourself tea. eyes closed, you compress yourself into an infant & catch yourself crying. because you got yourself water w/out begging. because the doctors cast you out the garden of simple cures. like a secret you find at the bottom of a prayer, you discover a mass that was twisted by your history: the back bone connected to the heart of hate, neck hollowed out from urban stress, jaw locked in teeth grinding at night. lumps of hurt, clumps of fear in your stomach you were told to hold in. tricks. i did as i was told & look where it got me.

the first vision of healing is a flash that fills in your life w/ excited chatter. i'm gonna be okay you think, all i have to do is calm down & change completely. all i have to do is relax & create trust & learn how to breathe w/out passion.

you get religious. god as crutch & comforter. god as a fleshy place away from revolutionary causes. prayers so simple they set you apart from your world view & shrink you to peanut size: your wish list distills down to quiet. you dig out a path of comfort through all cells of consciousness, the first cut into the rain forest w/ sadness in place. you visualize women in blue & purple work clothes w/ sponges & water bottles who clean up the mess, lubricate your organs & fix it.

then time asserts its hold on the world & you wear out. the loneliness of healing loops, the solitude of suffering recycles when the hurt returns. pain severs sweetness from your nervous system. pain slices joy out your body language. humor fades & fills in w/ a brutal sky, white & domineering. the bitch takes over & she's worse than cranky, worse than lost, an abandoned baby, her eyeducts are wide w/ extra moisture & love of tantrums, you are always ready to cry. like a strength you are stealing, each time you find your way back to original hope, flashing & full of primal patience, you take oaths of marriage to yourself.

air tightens around you like a glove, the special present of a body bag god made for you alone. you understand the message of the solitary dream, the desert marx never thought of, pan africanists forgot to claim, a space cleared between political theories & personal worship where no one comes near you, trapped inside the mystery of a failing body, where no one can come close & share transformation of the pain.

Solitude Ain't Loneliness

Say for instance you're a girl/   but citified/   a hard sister
like to keep her eyes open when she fucks/   & carries weapons
for the urban night creatures on the prowl/   Say you ain't
got no freudian thing/   but you packing none the less:
        your mucous is acid
        your anger on a leash
& can't no wish from the mouth of a warm eyed boy
make you blink

Before the girl mist can enter you/   before you ever cop
a feminine buss/   & blow the urban rust out your uterus
        you got to clear house
        you got to clean out
all the greasy fuzz/   left behind by the rat pack lot
of ex-lovers

You got to celibate/   in silence
& wait & wait for a red blush to rise up
a sparkling rush as radical as your first blood
as muscular as your momma's hands in soapy water
cold as the shock of the first breath
the earth blew into your lungs

The black sky wants your ass purified
& clear enough to release this city's fear
free enough to close your eyes
go inside & hear her.

Howl for White Negroes

Sometimes I be like miss bad ass black chick
                              above & beyond anything
left behind by some white men.
                    Sometimes honky culture piss me off & wear me out
'cept when I'm checking out the beats
            the bongo drum beats of the old-time beatniks
                              & their pseudo jazz
scene, hey, truth is, I'm into it.
                    Truth is them wine-drinking poet-types
the knapsack-lugging, zen-meditating poem writers
                              give me a literary tradition
a language of resistance
            & bongos
                    give me hope & spit & joyful ways to
avoid all that fearful tap dancing
            that assimilation got the heart of the mainstream
that lie-eating, lie-generating life style
            that makes this breathing process deathly boring.

Problem is we ain't got no name
                    for the scene of this age. We not hippies
we not beatniks
we got a touch of the punk
                    but the heck w/ giving punk the leadership.
Punk ain't got the spunk
            not the spark
            ain't got the know w/ all insight
to righteously dish out the dirt
                    to the yuppie, bluppie, guppie materialist
sell-outs in this girl's city.
                    It's a buncha lames out there
a buncha car-washing dead butt squares who has given up
                    hope of all magic & meaning in life
except from what comes from things.
                        Things like delirious automobiles.
Things like pajamas & 52 pairs of shoes.
                    I myself drive a dented toyota
take me every place but space
            & hey, ferlinghetti take me there.
            Where I let my finger pop & black kaufman's lead

my eyes & hands dig me way out there
                    where it's happening.
            I'm a believer.
                                I'm a bohemian believer
into the scholarly seeking of poetic self-worth.
                    And if you're into it
                            BE INTO IT, I say
& be hip to getting the magic to swell
                    from the mind to the page to the air
in the beatnik tradition of jack
                    bongo beating, black-wearing jack kerouac

Yes lord, mr. k's pissed me off
                    w/ they misogyny & drinking w/ the pigs
& the intrinsic limitation of a white vision
                            but me & my black hands
we not prejudice.
            Everywhere we go we seeks us a lesson of crazy wisdom
                                    we take us a lesson
from the white boy prince of the bums:

Keep faith in coolness.
            Stay wildly in love.
                        Always seek & sacrifice for the poem
hey
what could be better
than that?

it's them flat
>flat
>flat flat freeways
that make you think of old lovers
& make you wish for music
& settle for solo singing
it's them palm trees poking through the blue
& the sweat that puts a chill
on hot ass lost angeles
when the animals go to the beach
& forget about germany & babies & trouble
it's quiet except for the whoosh
& when people go off
& fist up at the mini malls
flip you off on the road
it's a fast food chicken sandwich
i stuff in w/ one hand
all the fastest streets on the west side
i put gas in my pacifist ride
& don't never have to talk to no one
broken radio, so what
alone it ain't but one key
& i can sing in it
it's them short cuts
before & after the jammed up right
time crunching nerve munching
traffic tied up person
the actual human being
trapped in this shit
it's the poison-us grit
that burned out bad attitude
frozen in the physics of l.a.
& the generous colors of our sky
when it ain't brown or yellow
like piss or beer.
it's cold.   it's funky.
i live here.

We're All Gringos on this Bus / Ode to the Am. Butch

judy the straight girl
showed me mexico
taking into account i hate
traveling/ traveling
to me is mostly about eating in cafes
having servants
& collecting rip-off stories
to flash your interesting-ness
& your excess cash worth
like:
      i ate eyeballs in thailand
      i got robbed in europe
      i lucked up at the airport in jamaica
      & found a sucker who put me up for days
      got me fully drugged
      & showed me how to beat native prices

like you pack up your gringo power
pay pennies for religious artifacts
overlook mutilated beggars
& fail to take note
of racism

you take like the mexico
judy the straight girl gave to me
was about dark skinned people
removing the plates & hand
washing our underpants while
white mexicans pick up the cash

plus time lays out like a woman
what-to-do is a list that struggles
w/ i-need-a-nap burn out
& mostly i get scared
because what do i know about traveling

judy, bi-cultural jewish
homie, hetero sexual to the max
details of her man addiction
would gag a political dyke
had straight people confusion anyway
even though she had that feeling

about that thing
she figured she should think about women
i mean like think about thinking about
ideas about intercourse w/ women
even though she never had a crush on a girl
not once kissing lessons in the tomboy club
& no appreciation for butches

so girlfriend i says to judy
on the mexican bus
where hopefully nobody speaks english
let me hip you to the american butch
it's their boots
it's their motorcycles
it's the way they take basketballs
away from men

to me there's four categories of humans
you're bi-lingual, i'm bi-sexual
you got your boys
good for certain kinds of deliciousness
you got straight girls like yourself
i never touch
lesbians who scare me worse than traveling
& butches who look like drag queens
when they put on dresses
& manifest sexual powers
w/ or w/out penis imitation
censored by american porn

judy pulled her face back
like i was taking up too much air
& crossed her eyes like
no capiche, no comprendo
this aspect of collective consciousness
is not in my head space
i was thinking about thinking about
thoughts of improved emotional
communication w/ girls
i wasn't talking about fucking
men thrill & hypnotize me
w/ hard body language
& that freudian thing
i just like closeness w/ my girl
friends better

yo judy, i tried to hip her
that ain't love-based erotica
that ain't mysterious forces
that get us in bed, in relationship
w/ god knows who

hell we in mexico
we out here traveling
like we own the world
i seen your titties
you talk about my tacky bras
& ain't no desire to it
that's buddyship & sharing fascination

w/ no interior impulse
no use trying to play
w/ dangerous forces
inside wild gay territory
it's the fourth fucking dimension
it takes more than an airline ticket
costs more than straight girl double
language smarts can secure
will take you to places of foreign knowledge
w/out a buss pass
w/out a easy frame of reference
w/out the heart to recognize
anything you used to think
was home.

Last Daze in Church in Mexico

My friend Enrique drinks mescal for the jelly-less vertebrae in his back. Good, clear, bootleg alcohol that numbs the pain that comes w/ the cold in mexico. "If it is a bad day," he tells me as he lays down his tools & lines up his paints, "the drink helps me remember the air itself is innocent."

The blue bandanna is the blue eyes he looks through when he mixes the new color for the old saints he restores. The doves make a sound like fire, the wild bird's crackle blurs w/ the mexican radio, a mix-up of natural & electric sounds that reminds me of the city, of urban violence, what Enrique warns me about: my kin from the city, my kind, the tree killers & lovers of cash. I grin because I know he lies. I hit the mescal because I feel tickled.

All around us the gods are bleeding, all the saints too old to recognize, so I think of flesh: Enrique's hands, my tongue, & the hearts of the dead artisans who propelled their suffering through wood & paint so long ago, their lives hung on stained sticks, inside sexless men rotting in robes. That time spread out & decayed, letting the children grow & give birth, grow & give birth again, until we grew into an age of humans who murder trees for toothpicks & ruin the earth. The descendants pump the soil w/ chemical nutrients that force up a sweet corn. "Next year," says Enrique, "next years the land will be useless & in May the flowers are dried & gray."

He tells me I am a thief, trying to make money from the words of an old art restorer. "No," I say, "I make no money from my art." "Ahh, the bourgeois privilege of those who can do what they want." I show my teeth. I pop my fingers.

My face is pasted w/ the color of the big continent, the glow in my
   mouth is the mean music of african slaves transformed on
   american dirt. I am tall, I am nigguh power they call gringa
   negra, so I snap my fingers & let my face break in wide grins.
Enrique is white: pure aryan, w/ azure eyes & the german bone
   structure born to the twisted history of eastern europe. He
   escaped, built this church & a museum in Pottsquarro where he
   remakes latin artifacts. He says he has never known home. I am
   dark & displaced. He speaks five languages. I watch him drink.
"Foolish priests," he says, his words beginning to slur, "tricked by
   tunes & the precision of language," & I don't get his meaning
   though I agree, priests are foolish. "Notice the different character
   of our creations," he continues & the face he paints fills in w/ a
   look cleanly human, sharply sad, made from a murdered tree.
   "Notice the balance in the work of the spaniards, all these thick
   robes stable on two small feet." His iron tools scrape color, tools
   made from metals to imitate the strokes of the dead spaniards.
   "You can trust machines," he says, "but you cannot trust the
   people who believe in machines."
He tells me the saints whisper to him: "You faithless creature," they
   say, so I pour him another shot of the bootleg mescal & pop
   my fingers. "The hard day exists w/out an intention to beat us
   down," he says as he works like an ant w/ no sense of time.
   "A great heart beats in this old wood but she will not weep," he
   goes on. "The goddess will return for rejuvenation & revenge,"
   he swears as he lifts the green glass to the edge of his lips &
   sucks. Wobbling & red eyed, he packs his tools in preparation
   to at last leave the church.

Outside the coldness of mexico thins to a heated white sky, the church opens underneath a stone sun, not smiling, & a moon w/ closed eyes. The yellow flowers of wild squash accompany the graves in the corner of the yard. Here the dead lay under square roots & small rocks, hand layered & trouble to my feet. Here Enrique made an archway from mud, the leaves of the black trees hover over us like a swarm of indifferent bees. Mexicans, a woman & a child, saw me cursing their jesus on my way out, but I didn't see them. Finally, eyes turned away from the black & blue mountains of god, we wave goodbye, but they say nothing.

Chronic Fatigue Syndrome
prologue

there is a down side of life & everybody knows it
 beware long term busters & the hard crash of illegal drugs
 beware depression bummers & 28 bad days in a row
 watch out your head tips off & steel toe boots
  stomp mush out of your feelers
so what
this is new news to no one
this is the same ole same old
 one dimensional rhetoric of thangs past
advice that don't get you off
or maximize your flight once you buzzing

there is a hassled part of existence & we know what to do:
 share a shower or a condom
 take your pick
 chocolate, pork rinds or kundalini sex rite
 fess up your miseries to the eternal living journal
 or funnel troubled hallucinations to a human ear
  if you don't have a cat
& if that don't work, feel free
to lean on
 scientifically generated psychiatrically distributed
 anti-depressants w/ only minor side effects
 like cotton mouth & delayed orgasm
so what

so what if the opposite happens
if happiness & meaning & future tense joy
 wraps her legs around you & comes
& you feel like coffee & bennies & pharmaceutical speed
 but you ain't had none
say the divine principle of light visits your apartment
 & makes a list of things for you to do
 & you do it all
your payback is big time know how & vision:

you see the post-modern multi-cultural revolution
 vibrating in the future
you sense all white folks eventually blur w/ misc. coloreds
 so traces of europeans survive only in museums

pretty neat, huh?
& class-ass struggle disintegrates w/ a pillow fight
        in the den of free market boogie men
& the evil menace of dick brained men & their uncle tom women
        get hit w/ a politically correct virus
        & die out quick like
& the vegetarians work it out w/ the burger lovers
& the earth shakes off the plastic
        in a final quake of self worship
& we have peace
        except it's generations ahead
this makes you happy
this makes you think
        you don't need sleep
        you ain't scared to die no more
        & pain don't hurt

this is a problem of a different order
this is the secret sin of hyped-up visionaries
        the inner sanctum of alienated weirdos
this is the manic maniac buzz that threatens
        your biochemical center w/ chronic burn out
        hospitalization & death
your separation from the physical is the glitch
        of a well-fueled mind
        the final refuge of the neo-politicized nerd

you better watch out
better drink herbal teas & master meditation
better pace that vision & stay cozy w/ your comforter
& keep planted in the gut of personal emotion
sure you wanna be a god
        fuse all cultural systems into one
        good time trip for all the peoples
but you ain't jesus
real gods don't go crazy

you are a twinkle of dust that touches everything
        your death diminishes all time
        your detachment from sensation
                sorrows the source of all life

so better keep the body precious & rested
keep close to the sleep process

& remember to get upset w/ real problems in real time
better keep the juicy pulse that flushes
  a happening body

take care
stay hooked up
plugged in
& caring.

Why Black Dinosaurs Will Always Be Cool

my father gave me my grandfather just like my momma gave me me/
in a weird way/   an emptiness created by blood/   in a way that ties &
splits me open w/ wonder/   cause i never knew him/   two generations
of patriarchs swallowed by male silence/   it is a hard journey to know
you never knew the men folks/   another post modern installment of
wretched alienation & loneliness/   i rode in an airplane through the
particled sky of los angeles/   to say goodbye/   to face the scars &
mythology of the man who made my father a man/

who sat in a bulky chair/   dissolving himself in whiskey/   a booze so
brown it soothed him behind the haze in his eyes/   that slow steady
drinking/   jump started in the morning/   not drinking like he wanted
to get drunk/   or a quick kick to light up dancing/   that slow steady
swallow like you gotta numb out the beast on your back/   that delayed
tranquilizer for rage in the bone marrow/   sipping a shot glass you
never see the bottom of/   won't get violent/   won't pass out/   just a
shield against monsters w/ boots & implements of psychic destruction/
yo pops/   daddy of the daddy of the world/

what my father told me about you: from a family of twenty-two children
& dirt floor/   the first of our line to graduate high school/   plus two
years college/   who washed bottles & hosed down the yards of white
folks/   no real jobs for educated darkies/   any hustle for a quarter/
friend of the colored dentist & the colored criminal/   unofficial high
counselor for the personal plagues on working class negroes/   men
loved his quiet eyes/   did tax returns for pimps/   could arrange
abortions/   money wasn't no solution/   refused the church/   refused

to say the word nigger/   came in late & left early/   any hustle for a dime/   always tired but never sick/   refused the splits caused by divorces in the clan/   you are my people/   respected by even the color struck catholic matriarchs/   always two jobs plus & the sense to marry a woman who could work like an animal & like it/   beat his sons & spoiled his daughters/   took in stray children/   we took care of our own back then/   we took care/

what my momma said: he wouldn't talk/   just like your father/   he would come home & not even speak to his family/   all grumpy & mean & worn down from working/   he'd eat his dinner & pass out on the couch/

the other thing my mother said: he grabbed my titties in the kitchen/ he walked up behind me & grabbed me/   here/   like this/   your father was off at college/   i had nowhere to go/   so i couldn't do nothing/

what i wonder: did you ever know a klans man/   was anybody lynched/   were you spit on/   cursed as wicked & diseased/   did you feel like an animal/   are white women ugly to you/   did philosophy reject you while you did the dirt work of white people/   did your mind ever turn on you/   did you lose your body in your dreams/   did you think of god/   did you think of the devil/   how did you shape your prayers/   what did it feel like to beat a male child/   how can you love all black people/   why did you touch my momma like that/ you must have known it was wrong/   why are you drinking grandpa/ why do you drink/

before he died he came to los angeles to say goodbye to me/   his skull packed w/ stories of the white man's evil/   like maybe i should dig out the roots/   w/ a tape recorder & spiral notebook & pass it on to the youth/   but he is all the body of a black silence/   denial as a twisted strength/   a worn down patriarch dissolving himself in alcohol/   history compressed in his body language/   the slump in his spine/   the red lumps & cataract over his field of vision like mucus/   the shine on the leather/   the leather of skin/   of self/   passive as a brown ghost/ i step on my grandfather's memory & think/   you are cool old man/ i won't never give you a hard time/   except for that shit about my momma/   i don't give you a hard time/

Healing Madness Healing Magic

Are you ready to be healed
     do you think you ready to be healed
you know you need it
we all need it
     it ain't a soul in this place couldn't use some healing
but the question is not do you need it
     the question is have you prepared
have you got up off the walls
     have you torn down your protection
     & set fire to denial
     have you burned w/ the heat
     that first made you hurt
are you intimate w/ your scar tissue
     have you sobered up w/ the first step
it's your job to dig out the infection
     reacquaint yourself w/ the pus
     & activate the powers of the demons you swallowed
i'm talking about a slow, steady opening of the wounds
     a careful undoing of the plastic stitches

you, i'm talking to you
     you act like some magic pill
     some hypno-therapist w/ a herbal recipe
     & a new age rap
     can snap her fingers
     & put you back in the womb
     & restore a cosby childhood of ignorance & privilege
shit
     this ain't fast food
     this ain't no cruise ship to jamaica
     this ain't no easy out to cocaine bliss
     or an orgasm w/ no responsibilities
we wish it was as easy as a drug
     as quick as laser surgery & fax machines
     we wish you only had to do it once
i'm here to tell you
     this is a life long process
     of work & hurt & comfort

is it any healers out there
    besides folks who have done the work
    & are ready to be healed
    we need us some healers
    we need us some grown up girls & boys
    who can come on w/ it
    & wanna give up some human help
    is it folks here w/ living hearts
fools america ain't whipped yet
    or made selfish & anemic
anyone ready to name & confront evil
we need us some brothers of courage
    not no red badge of courage
    not no go to war & kill a stranger courage
    not no ready for battle w/ men on the other team courage
i'm looking for brothers
    who wanna name & disembowel the hard evil
    that tried to ruin so many of us
we need the selfless heartbeat of a healthy father
the eyes & hands of a birth mother

understand. this ain't no easy job
this ain't light weight activity
    this will terrorize your ass w/ the salt of sweat
    & the burn of vicious memories
    healers got to come across w/ the big heart action
    healers got to get up off some energy
how we gonna ask folks to speak
    if ain't nobody listening
how we gonna ask folks to open up
    & be for real inside a hollow void
    made by the money loving dead spirit
    anti-fuck of this world

i'm asking you to be the foundation of a changing community
    the rock
    the keepers of the first honest word
    the house frame built on the good dark earth
you generous & beautified healers
    for a time got to forget your personal needs
it's a lot about listening
    it's a lot about absorption
    it's about keeping your eyes open

    & no blinks, no lazy blindness
    & hearing, however horrible, the whole ordeal
like you doing now

it's about sharing your heart beat
the music that is ours
it's about rocking
it's about
together we
can be
whole.

Manifesting the Girl Hero

Yo girl hero
i'm standing at the edge of this patriarchal situation
      & you know i got a problem
i'm looking up at the dick like monster building
      of westwood & hollywood & brentwood
      where men w/ no neck do they dirty business
      & you know i might get depressed
i'm at the end of urban l.a.
      where the dirty air of america
      greets the oily ocean of our world
      & i'm saying
i can not get a grip
my good humor is in jeopardy
      cause the boy hero done had his way
      & built this cold ass madness
so i'm putting you on notice
i'm calling you out
yo girl hero
i'm forming you up
      like you was mud & i am powers that be
i'm scraping you off the inside of the television eye
the girl whose goods get the job done
the bitch whose blood pours
      into the void & heals it
      seeps into the wound & seals it
& the girl ain't no angel
she ain't no soup cooking momma
      w/ bible & generous breasts
you can't suckle relief from her body
because the girl hero got a problem
she is the wrath of the brutalized vagina
& she don't understand like a woman
she ain't listening like your momma
she prefers masturbation to the fuck
      of the slave arrangement called romance & the family
her lips don't part in a smile of anger
& she don't satisfy easy.

Giving Up the Near-Sighted Ghost /
In Praise of the Multi-Cultural

i breathe in a multi-cultural world wind/   i spread out the third world eye/   black bits at the base of a global experience/   sacred spectrum of wet colors & earth

i used to be one dimensional/   one girl, one father, no homeland/ then discourse w/ asia made me free/   i embrace a taoist contradiction/ i'm a african thing & a black thing & a colored thing & a vaginal thing & a human/   being a thing born to break traps of single-lensed identity/

i used to be black in a vacuum of two colors/   then somebody brown yelled somebody yellow/   you half breed, you oreo, you wanna be, you ain't quite the right shade/   somebody mixed brought in the same shape of pain/

i walk on international earth ground/   bilingual & optimistic about the first word/   hold the tongue loose for a real latin sound/   musica negra de mujeres y hermanas/   asian ritual as gifts in my mouth/   rice balls the size of the pacifist fist/

i used to be trapped in a fight w/ the opposite color/   then a cool white boy shared his despair/   then a jew gave me nine drops of wine/ then a blonde self-mutilated her internalized hate/   & i thought/ enough is enough/   really/   i mean do i want to beat up these people/ traumatize their off spring/   revenge is a chain to warfare in the future/ hell i can swallow/   i can stop/

once i lived inside the fight w/ the dead white folks/   not like the problem is gone/   hear me right/   forgiveness does not mean forgotten/ some people choose a nazi/   some folks build space around hate/

but i burn for the flame of all color/   we are not children of a good time/   not babies of a loved breast/   our splits are vaginal & blistered/ our scars are wars of hard histories/

so everybody knows this shit/   the japanese know about bombs/   the gays know about silence/   armenians appreciate ghosts/   the five nations understand extinction/   the women know about still born, butchered, buried contractions that screamed for birth & died anyway/ & americans know about lies/   black hands grip the wisdom of your suffering
that is mine
that is african   that i give you

the echo of feminists kiss souls in exile/   you got a momma/   you ain't no stranger/   a woman gave birth to a woman who gave birth to a woman who gave birth to this ideal party for mourners/   an ideal party for mourners of the broken bond/   we grieve the big bang rape/

but the earth is a stubborn bitch/   her old ass spirals in light that expands/   that will out live the rain of greedy violence/   that will bury our plastic mutations/   that feeds on the death of material fixation/ evil biodegrades/   cruelty is the sum of its infantile parts/   the fat mother reclaims her own in the end/

i breathe in a multi-cultural world wind/   i spread out the third world eye/   black bits at the base of a global experience/   sacred spectrum of wet colors & earth/

i swim in the poly-racial birth-place/   the uterus as universe of blood/ red placenta that cradles the origin/   the root: my people are your people are all people/   we break w/ the waters of the tribe/   we make family as big as the earth/

Warrior Council

the time in the cave was time well spent
    our girl hero is born
    the dark & the soil
    the perfect molecular spark
    to start off the live baby girl
    her mouth sucked in voices
    her eyes as mirror shine
    dumb as a duck that copied
    clean as a fax machine
    xeroxes of her parents' time

it's a trap, you know, we are all born into a trap
    all infants dwarfed by the cathedrals of culture
    like the fossils of dinosaurs too big to rot
    monuments of 'how we do things around here
    how we gonna keep doing things
    & how you, sweet baby girl, will fit exactly
    see these pink booties
    change this plastic dollie
    she wets, she pees
    don't squat when you play marbles
    you're not a boy you know
    practice dress up
    you're so cute
    like a bunny, like a declawed cat, an angel on a diet
    we enjoy looking at you
    but cover up that messy opening: keep your ankles tight
    don't let that smell get out'

the inner world of the self
    cradled in the home front of the family
    all she needed was sweet & sour breast milk
    & sleeping & passing gas
    the harsh light she fell into
    warned her she was really a hero
    even if the blanket was pink
    prepare for assault
    the home front had sneaky ways
    creepy ways of entering your body
    & colonizing your thinking space

the first atrocity was the abomination of the man of kin
        the exiled man who grew ugly
        outside the nest of child rearing
        whose sadness mutated into an evil
        too gross to look at
        whose cloak was the language of secrets
        his power the silence of dysfunction
        the first atrocity was penetration by flesh of kin
        he molested her, or incested her, or raped her,
        she confessed twenty years later on the oprah winfrey show
        i thought he was peeing in my mouth
        while donahue & montel & sally jessy rafael
        said across the national head waves
        you need a good cry
        you could use a session w/ therapy man

backwards in time the patriarchal head waves told our girl hero
        you don't need to fight
        you're too pretty to make a fist
        too weak to pick up a weapon
        to sweet to use the evil eye
        cause daddy will protect you
        brothers will guard you
        plus law man & jesus man shelter you from harshness

the second atrocity is the man of love gone crazy w/ rage
        the beatings inside domestic boundaries
        the wine glass broken & inserted
        knife man eats dinner w/ the frustrated spouse
        the stranger who stalks wants to be in the movies
        somebody thinks fear is sexy
        some liar feeds lies to these men

the third atrocity is the cavern of fear for females
        freezing us into victim-ness
        the swamps of bad movies
        w/ frailty & terror as sexy girl stars
        we run — we're always captured
        we scream — they gag our fight
        the final atrocity is what is left in our minds
        timid skinny women
        incapable of self-defense

sister cousins of the girl hero picked up their teeth
        & organized training camps of women

ready for gun defense
ready to stop whining & weeping
ready for prayers to the goddess of war
armies of women body guards & women psychics
sent out the subversive message
it's good to take a stance
our lady of the swift kick
it's right to land a tight fist in the throat of male aggressors
the pacifism of good girls is weak as an open window
to a deranged man

i just wanna tell you about the girl hero
the colors in her meditation practices
always blue & black & red
for the dead women behind us
the wounded woman inside us
i just want you to know about the girl hero
the water she breaks when she prays
the fear she defeats w/ self-love ritual
her muscles tough & not angry
her heart prepared to punch target
the fist feminine & clenched
hear now about the girl hero
the woman who calms inner violence
the woman centered in her breath
the quiet she loves in darkness
i just want a walk on the beach at night
i just want to trust strangers & smile for anybody
i want to be forgiven all history, all personal hurt
i want you to know there is a girl hero
a woman who will fight
a woman who defends the peace centers
who wants quiet & fun & healthy lovers
she is pure as an animal
ancient as death & mourning
the mythology she writes
the vision she reads by renegade women mystics
we uncover healers & muscular mothers & warriors who sing
we re-write the word of the universe
w/ power women w/ power weapons
that a woman's love
grows w/ combat knowledge:

know your enemy as you know yourself
resist assault
resist psychic death as you find yourself

i just want you to know about the girl hero's need for peace
i want the globe to birth open safe places for her feet

The following poems were developed & performed as text for performance art:

"Blood is a Bright Color & Tears Are Clear"
"Traditional Post-Modern Neo-HooDoo Afra-Centric Sister
     in a Purple Head Rag Mourning Death & Cooking"
"Cubist Poem: Momma Read It Right"
"Uterus Root"

> Black August; in collaboration w/ Keith Antar Mason, directed by Susan Carpendale; Beyond Baroque, August 1988

"Anti-Erotica"

> with Ruben Martinez; Erotica Night; Beyond Baroque, February 1990

"Sensei Maria's Story"
"Manifesting the Girl Hero"

> First Annual Girl Hero Happening & Tho Down; Highways Performance Space, May 1990

"Politics of the Bisexual Deep Fry"

> Lesbian Erotica Cabaret; Highways Performance Space, July 1991

"Healing Madness Healing Magic"

> Dissections; conceived by Akilah Nayo Oliver, directed by Keith Antar Mason; Highways Performance Space, December 1991

"Warrior Council"

> collaboration with Linda Frye Burnham, G. Colette Jackson, Dan Kwong, Francisco Letelier, Keith Antar Mason; Highways Performance Space, November 1992